THE B*EASTS

by Monica Dolan

SAMUEL FRENCH

samuelfrench.co.uk

 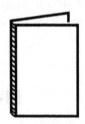

Bush
Theatre
We make theatre for London. Now.

The Bush is a world-famous home for new plays
and an internationally renowned champion of
playwrights. We discover, nurture and produce
the best new writers from the widest range of
backgrounds from our home in a distinctive corner
of west London.

The Bush has won over 100 awards and developed
an enviable reputation for touring its acclaimed
productions nationally and internationally.

We are excited by exceptional new voices,
stories and perspectives – particularly those with
contemporary bite which reflect the vibrancy of
British culture now.

Located in the newly renovated old library on
Uxbridge Road in the heart of Shepherd's Bush,
the theatre houses two performance spaces, a
rehearsal room and the lively Library Bar.

 Supported by
ARTS COUNCIL
ENGLAND
 h&f
hammersmith & fulham

bushtheatre.co.uk

ABOUT THE AUTHOR

Monica Dolan is a British/Irish citizen who was born in Middlesbrough and brought up in Woking. She trained at the Guildhall School of Music and Drama and has been working as an actress for over twenty years. In 2012 she won a BAFTA for her role as Rosemary West in the TV drama *Appropriate Adult*, and is otherwise best known for *Alan Partridge: Alpha Papa*, *W1A*, *The Falling*, *The Arbor* and *Eye in the Sky*. She has done extensive theatre work with the Royal Court Theatre, the National Theatre, the RSC, Shared Experience, and Out of Joint.

Monica co-wrote *Underbelly*, which won the London New Plays Festival in 1998, and is currently developing a four-part historical drama for television with Trevor Bentham and Snowed-In Productions. She won The Stage Edinburgh Award 2017 for Outstanding Performance in *The B*easts* at the Festival Fringe.

She lives in Hammersmith.

AUTHOR'S NOTE

At the end of an early reading of *The B*easts*, the first question at the hosting theatre came from the young education representative. Was *The B*easts* a true story? I was astonished. I almost laughed. No, I said, of course not! She then told me that as part of her recent outreach work, she had visited some schools in Manchester. A common question she had been asked by many of the female pupils, she said, was how old you have to be to get a boob job.

Was some of *The B*easts* too strong, too shocking? I asked. No, she said, because we are so immersed in a rape culture.

We have seen padded bras and bikinis for seven-, eight- and nine-year-olds come and go from Matalan and Primark, kids' pole-dancing kits from Tesco and the sale of shoes with heels for little girls still resolutely defended by Next and Gap, on the grounds that they sell. Which seems to have become a good – if not the only – reason for anything. And David Cameron emphasising that the responsibility for these things must be with companies and retailers themselves, and any legislation and accountability lying with government is not the answer.

Since writing, we have seen Katie Price vilified in the press and social media for posting a picture of her nine-year-old daughter, made-up, in a pouty and provocative pose, where the child appears more like a young woman in her late teens. Katie is someone who left school and started out working in a care home and then training as a nurse. By "morphing" into Jordan, she became rewarded by society in every possible way for the heightened celebrity sexualisation of herself. Now, somehow, when it comes to "maximising" her daughter's "potential", we are surprised at her behaviour and disgusted. Somehow we expect a miracle of instant amnesia of past survival and business experience in a person the moment she becomes a mother.

With companies exploiting a loophole to target engagement with children on the internet, we have seen the sneaky rise of "advergames", where a cute product-related character is put in an online game for children to play, thereby increasing – and prolonging – the child's engagement with the advertising and product, while the child is seldom aware that what they are engaging with is an advert at all. Brands interact directly with kids on Facebook.

There are no age regulations on cosmetic procedures for children except in relation to tanning or tattoos, and nothing to protect them from the cosmetics industry. So we now have online games that promote cosmetic procedures like botox for the under eighteens – "Plastic Surgery Princess" and "Pimp My Face" – many are plastic surgery simulators that show children how their bodies can be altered. Makeover apps and Cosmetic Surgery games target children as young as nine.

The news has reported the criminal acts of surgeon Ian Paterson – in Britain – performing unnecessary mastectomies in the public and private health arena, and mutilating patients for personal grandeur and financial gain.

Breast enhancement is advertised pre-watershed on television during *Dinner Date*.

So, yes, all of the elements necessary for *The B*easts* to be a reality, seem to me to be in waiting and in place. But, as with many of our problems that have gone before, no doubt we will sleepwalk into the normality of them until – should we still be equipped to notice it – we see some effect on a middle-class child.

Monica Dolan
July 2017

In this latest edition I have included notes at the end depicting the cuts and changes I made for the Edinburgh Fringe version of *The B*easts*, which had to be an hour long. These, or a selection of these, are cuts I suggest for those who want to present a shorter version of the play.

Monica Dolan
February 2018

"The great ambition of women is to inspire love"

Molière

The B*easts was first produced by Suzanna Rosenthal for Something For The Weekend, and previewed at the Etcetera and the Bush Theatre before premiering on 5 August 2017 at the Big Belly, Underbelly, Cowgate, at the Edinburgh Festival Fringe 2017. It had its London premiere at the Bush Theatre on 12 February 2018.

TESSA Monica Dolan

Director – John Hoggarth

Designer – James Button

Lighting Design – Tom Clutterbuck

Company Stage Manager – Rebecca Maltby

This script went to press during rehearsals, and may differ from the text in performance.

CHARACTERS

TESSA – is a woman in her forties. She is a psychotherapist. Earthed, empathic, intelligent, neutral, sharp, dry, caring.

Special thanks to

Jonathan Holloway, Toby Whithouse, Joanna Griffin, Zoe Boyle, Nick Payne, Marc Wootton, Jacqui Somerville and Mountview Theatre School, Nadine Rennie, James Button, Alan Harris, Jenny Van Der Lande, Rebecca Maltby, Ann Dolan, Paul Dolan, Madani Younis, Stewart Pringle and all at The Bush, John Hoggarth, Ria Parry, North Wall Arts Centre, Woking Library, Shepherds Bush Library, Suzanna Rosenthal and all at SFTW, Chris Lincé, Tom Clutterbuck, Sean Holmes, Imogen Kinchin and all at the Lyric Hammersmith, Laura Rourke, Will Hollinshead, Livi Shean, Tish Jones, Chloé Nelkin, Tilly Wilson, Helen Atkinson-Wood, Wendy Nottingham, Lara Stubbs, Louise Breckon Richards and Sarah Ball.

For My Family

In the dark, TESSA *is on the phone.*

TESSA *(message)* Oh Ali, it's me. I think you're playing five-a-side. Look, just... I'm just leaving a message because I think your dad's left his phone off, so just in case you happen to see him. Just get him to call me. Bye, darling.

As the lights come up TESSA *hangs up and puts her phone in her bag. She sits on a chair with a small table beside. It has a glass of what looks like whisky and an electronic cigarette, which she screws in and starts smoking.*

Mmm. Don't often get time for a break. Having more these days. Having to. Make space for them. Well, these are good *(referring to the e-cigarette)*. I didn't actually smoke before really. I suppose if I was young there would be some debate about the advertising and whether that got me into it. Because everyone's protecting the young. Well, "meatily"* if not virtually. So yeah. These are meant to be good. I mean, they are good. There's a lot of talk about whether they are actually promoting them as a health thing over this side of the world in order to support the tobacco industry elsewhere. Because while the tobacco industry has its healthy cut of the healthy electronic market over here, cigarettes are being sold to kids in Africa. Their cigarettes. Sometimes one at a time. Supporting itself by looking good in one area. Fucking Peter to make love to Paul, you could say. It relies on having the life-long customer.

So yeah, it's just my way of relaxing really. You can't get all moral about it. Well, you can. I mean, I should be glad I'm doing this really. Could be doing yoga or something,

---

* This refers to "meat-space", which is cyber-speak for "the real world", the human space that we live in, as opposed to the "virtual" world or cyber space.

I suppose. But I mean, imagine what someone like me in all this has to do to relax? I've just been dealing with the mother. Where would they start? Does it look as if the child isn't inherently innocent and good? I mean, people are outraged by that. Something inside everyone balks at that. But then who's to say what she wanted was good or bad. I suppose it all comes down to just whether you think they are something filthy or whether they just are. Just there. Are they innocent? Do we have to look at ourselves and say, what have we done to make the child insist on this? We can't look at the child and say the child is to blame. If there is anything to be to blame for. That would ruin our notion of what innocence is. So we just blame the mother.

Sorry, I'm doing that thing that old people do, of coming up to you and starting talking about something in the middle of it and expecting you to know what I mean and then getting frustrated when you don't and not taking you through the first bit. Not very...clinical thing to do. Not very clear, but then, you know, I'm used to asking questions really. And making connections between the answers and making notes. That's my modus operandi. I don't often get like this. But yeah, so, I'll take you through. And maybe you'll make the connections and maybe you won't. I don't expect you to make notes.

So as you'll probably know, she didn't want to see me. Karen (we'll call her Karen – as you probably know, her name isn't anything like Karen, but we'll call her Karen) didn't want to see me. Well, she didn't initiate, didn't approach me. She had to see me after it all got so...big. I can see her point in not wanting to come. If she agrees to accept psychiatric help then that is to admit that she is, or has been in some way, ill. And I can see how there could be some debate about that. But everyone feels satisfied in some way if she agrees to see a psychotherapist, I suppose. The society doesn't want to punish her – can't punish her really – even though it loathes what she did, but it must acknowledge and separate what she did from the norm, so she has to come and see me. It doesn't want any more of what she did happening. Or not exactly what she did, but what she enabled. But then if a hundred businessmen decide that it could be the norm, who knows. Maybe it will be.

When she came, it had already got really big. You maybe know about it all anyway, but some of you might not, so I suppose I will tell you. She was very ragged the first time she arrived with me, Karen. Wouldn't talk for a while. And I used to do my usual of asking her what her thoughts were, what she had been thinking about when she was silent. And often she still wouldn't talk. I suppose that's what happens when you have been harangued by journalists and they have squeezed you dry, and undeniably it was a...story. I'm breaking doctor/patient confidentiality but I suppose, well... let's just say it's between you and me. I'm going to have to talk about this sometime. I will have to write another report. I will probably have to speak to the press or at least be quoted in the press at some point, and, who knows, if I ever start giving lectures, we'll call her Lila and Karen might be an important case study, or an experience for the novel, so...best if I process it with you. Why not. It's unusual for me too, you know. Unprecedented. I suppose the real point of interest is that it didn't happen in America first.

So. When I took Karen back to the beginning of it, when we started to try and examine everything, she told me that "call her Lila" was normal, had been a normal little girl. Strong-willed though. But that should be a good thing, shouldn't it? She was lively and intelligent. Precocious in some ways, Lila, according to Karen. Karen is her mum. Was her mum. I'm treating Karen, did I mention that? Because I have to. So, yeah, so. Lila's dad left them when she was about... two... That happens to lots of children, of course, though. Lila was...she was an only child and I suppose they looked at her – Karen looked at her in terms of being...lively. The disturbing thing for adults can be that children display what they – the adults – read as sexual or sexualised behaviour, but of course it is more complicated than that. The adults

are disturbed because they feel like a response is invited
in them, but, of course they suppress any impulse because
their protective instincts as a healthy adult, coupled with
their intellect, sees the wider picture, and this can come
out as what can be perceived by the child as a reprimand
or rejection. And, of course, in a simple way, flirting is an
important skill to learn and needs to be nurtured. It's one
of the ways people get on. Well. When I did a bit of digging
with Karen I did discover a couple of instances, where it
all started – or after it had already started a bit. Or started
enough for people to see. What you have to remember is
a lot of these things, these impulses, are healthy things,
but they just get distorted. Or maybe it's the world that
gets – is – distorted, but you see, it's my job to get people
to fit in with the world, distorted or not, so that they feel
happy. Or, not sad. Or...functioning. So, yeah, when I did
a bit of digging with Karen, she did remember a specific
one of these instances.

It was when Lila would have been about three and one of
her ex-husband's friends came to the house and you know,
this man, this friend, he had his own kids and everything
and he was – I suppose, the way Karen described it, he was
objectively sexy – he would have been like a Heathcliff or
Mr Rochester, "all man", troubled, should-have-been-and-
had-wanted-to-be-a-rock-star objectively sexy. I mean, the
Brontës would have been quite immature when it came
to sexual and marital relationships, so all the safely ideal
brutish, mannish, non-nice, love the "throw-down", caveman,
whip-me-beat-me-call-me-trash sort of man is on the
inside and on the out. Like it might be in a fantasy. So this
guy seemed a bit like that. What, if he was a woman, you
would call "available". Anyway, like I say, he was probably
slightly coming out the other side of realising he would
never be a rock star and starting to mourn it, and he was
at Karen's house and, the way she described it, the whole
thing was bewildering for him. He was sat down, just sat
on the sofa talking to Karen and then three-year-old Lila

comes in and she sees – she had never seen him before – and her mum introduces her and she starts hiding behind her mum but not really, really for his benefit, and then giggling and screeching and doing things to show off. She leaves the room then and comes back a few moments later in her plastic Dream Dazzler high heels and princess tutu, and then she lifts up her tutu a couple of times and shows him her pants, and he tries to carry on the conversation with Lila's mum and then she, Lila, she properly screeches and pants off and climbs on him and is bouncing on his lap and she's giggling in his face and Karen's just saying her name, half trying to get her to stop and half trying to ignore it, and the man, the not rock star friend, he is just aghast and bewildered and doesn't know how to respond. And then Karen described this to me and then described the man's response, which was as if Lila was a weirdo and a freak, somehow to blame, but then I took her through it again, I said, I asked her in the session if Lila's dad was inclined to ignore Lila, not look at her, start to not respond to her even before he left. And Karen went quiet. I could see her thinking back through times, seeing Lila's dad not looking at the child and snubbing her. So it – that – is not so not normal really, because if you are being ignored, you up the ante, don't you? To get to be noticed. And the girl's programming is to be desired. However, whenever that starts. Which seems to be an eternal matter for debate. It can happen healthily. Well, it used to.

So then, you know, time went by. There were probably more instances of it. The lively child, Karen trying to contain it, but Lila strong-willed and then witty at the same time, which can be difficult and shameful for a mum if you're trying to keep charge but your daughter is more intelligent than you. On examination, I discovered that even when he lived with them, Lila's dad would always have his chair pointing away from Lila, usually aimed at the TV. Or simply looking at his phone. Perhaps as if he was avoiding something. So. A man about the house pointing in her direction was a matter for celebration. A raven-haired, swarthy man with the embers of his inner rock star still glowing near the surface, a matter for euphoria.

Karen had always read magazines. No big deal. There had always been magazines in the house. I think we realise so little of how powerful our unconscious or subconscious is – and you can say, well, you would say that because that's what you read and work with, it's your stock-in-trade, but it's true. I mean, everyone knows that if someone you live with has a problem with something, the British "intervention" is to leave books about it lying around because they are bound to pick them up. Our environment is something that very powerfully goes into us, affects us. People used to say to a novelist friend, why have you got trains and railways all the way through all your work and, you know, she hadn't realised, hadn't consciously made it a motif, but she had been brought up in a commuter town near a station, and the trains were part of her emotional backdrop, so there you go. So yes, then if you want to add to that that you are dealing with a child, and that its experience of different environments is thus far limited but that its synapses are racing to multiply their journeys with accessing mounting information, then what is happening around them is a super-powerful, potent thing. It is their world. And, you know, some mums are too aware of it and hyper-control their children's environment and become really neurotic about it and then don't realise that that *neurosis* is part of the kid's environment too and they soak all that up too, and so their kids don't build up any immunity and end up being allergic to everything.

So Lila. She started to interact with the magazines. And, I mean, so far so normal. My niece went through a stage of reading the Argos catalogue for hours on end. But then I mean, she did end up going into advertising. She's one of those annoying people who emails you about Creme Eggs on Boxing Day. But the way Karen describes it, the way Lila would interact with the magazines, it was constant. All day. They would get taken away. She would run after them. Scream. Her attention would get diverted away, it would go back to them. And is it healthy? I mean, it's debatable. Women's magazines. Well, it's not debatable really. They're pretty unhealthy for women, they're pretty shit. And what are they going to do to a three-year-old who already has trouble attracting her dad? Her blueprint for the opposite sex? But let's not get too analytical, I'm getting ahead of myself here.

At first Karen thought she, Lila, was just pointing at the page. And, I mean that's what it would have looked like. Just a child ham-fistedly, unspecifically pawing at a random page, at a picture. You wouldn't particularly notice that what she was pointing at all had one thing in common. I mean, not unless you were looking. And not unless it became emphatic which, after a while, it did. And it's a cliché to say sex sells everything, and of course it does. I often wonder how long things have to be a cliché in order for any of us to do anything about them. If there's money involved, the answer is forever. It will always be a cliché. In fact, it then develops beyond a cliché. It becomes what's called a "universal truth", like "The poor are always with us". You see, I think we always knew that sex sells effectively, but now it has just got to the stage where we no longer feel confident to sell anything without it. Because the other fella might be. Karen and I have since looked through some of the magazines that would have been around at that time. And I mean, there's all the obvious usual sexualized stuff. But also other things. In one of the magazines was a soft-focus Chuka Umunna with the headline – "Could This Be Labour's New Leader?" It was pointed out how young he was – and implicitly eligible – but the thing that was, that was most noticeable was that he was smouldering at the camera. At the women. Unmistakably, he was selling himself. Sex for votes. Fantasise me. Want me. Vote for me. Vote with your C U Next Tuesday. So yeah, it goes on.

So. Another mother might have got rid of the magazines since they were what could be called "more than a diversion". I didn't say a "better" mother. Everyone has magazines. Don't they? She was entitled to her lifestyle. I'm not here to judge Karen. I'll leave that to the world I'm supposed to make her happy in. And then gradually Karen became aware that what it was was that Lila actually wanted something from the – in the magazines. She kept pointing to the page. She kept saying, "Want. Want that". A bit like that *Little Britain* character who kept saying "bitty" to his mum. What a grim comparison that is, actually. So she kept pointing; she knew what she wanted, like they do. And her mum would just get her to try and put the magazine down and she would scream. Start really screaming. Have tantrums. Throw herself around the bottom of the lounge, thrashing through violently-tossing curtains. I mean, what do you do? We all do it. We all use diversion tactics to stop that noise. Sometimes you just need the noise to stop – I mean it goes right through you, it's designed to. We've all given them an iPad. We've all given them something to shut them up. So Karen would give in. Of course she would give in. It was the only way to keep her, make her quiet – except it wouldn't make her quiet – she would get to a page, find a page and then find Karen and then point to the page, as if her finger were glued to the page. So small, she could barely hold the weight – some of those magazines have spines and are like books – but her whole small being was involved, she lived to hold that publication to her mum's attention, her whole being's energy inexorably aimed at a single parent.

And Karen would look, exasperated. Make placating sounds for her daughter. Try to get on with her own thing, which was rapidly no thing and no longer her own, try to work. Trying to see what secret the magazine held. Trying to fathom what her daughter wanted. Could possibly want. What could she possibly want? She paid attention, she tried to see a pattern. She saw a pattern. She began to guess when Lila grabbed a magazine like a ravenous octopus and raced through pages before she came to land, began to predict what the picture would be. And yes. The same picture, a pattern, began to turn up again and again. She must want a...the penny dropped. She wanted a bikini. But then one day during the familiar dance, the magazine was thrust at Karen and the woman in the picture wasn't wearing a bikini. She wasn't wearing anything on her top. And Lila was pointing to it. And Lila was saying, "Want, want". And Karen thought to herself still more forcefully that Lila wanted a bikini. Sometimes Lila would take the magazine and try to push against her mother's legs and push her over. And scream.

At other times, Lila would impersonate her mum, standing in a pouty 'S' shape with a curve in her back and a hand on her hip. But she would also reach her hands up to her mother, up for her breast, though she had long gone off it.

Oh, I should say, when Lila was just about four, she became brilliant at sexy dancing. It seemed slightly odd because it happened literally overnight – well, over a day. Lila's little friend had MTV at his house. The child Karen dropped off in the morning could do only little elbowy hands-and-knees and side-to-side dancing, and the child she went to pick up late that afternoon was rubbing down her torso with her imaginary long-fingernailed hands and grinding her figmental-thonged hips. I mean, in a way it shouldn't be odd because dancers can just learn dances, people can just pick up dances, ways of moving, can't they? And Lila had just picked it up off the telly. And at the time the mums had laughed! Karen and Lila's friend's mum had laughed because it was funny, because she was so good at it, and it looked like an idea. At least it did to them.

At school some of the little girls used to get embarrassed when they did papier mâché and some of the newspapers would have pictures of women with large bare chests, and some of the boys would go quiet and some would get excited and laugh and show them around to make the girls ashamed and make them hide. But Lila used to grab them off the

boys. She used to stare at them. She used to say, "I want
that one". And being at school now, of course, she could say
what she wanted. And this wasn't going away.

Karen was suffering under it. She was buckling under it.
She was listening. She was listening to her child's needs.
And yes, you can say I'm looking at it from Karen's point of
view. But that is the only point of view I have. Apart from my
own. It is the point of view I am working with. Maybe you
have seen some of those documentaries about transgender
kids. I think the Louis Theroux one won an award. And kids'
needs, and their identity. I suppose what I'm talking about
is responding to your child's needs. Your child's gender and
sexual identity needs. And their sexual identity has to be
decided and named fairly soon so that we as a society can
accept it and tell them it's ok. Even if it's a fluid identity.
That's ok too. In fact all sexual identity used to be fluid,
until you were married. His documentary was balanced and
we could see that if the child's gender identity that it felt
from within was other than its biological gender, it is more
straightforward to change the gender before puberty than
after puberty. Biologically. Because of the hormones. Not
that it was at all straightforward. So some of the children
were injected and treated before they became women or men,
so that they could grow into men or women. And I know, it
isn't the same, I know it isn't because she, Lila, was already
a girl, she didn't want to become a girl, and certainly not a
boy or a man. But maybe she wanted to become a woman.
Or a bit of a woman or have a bit of woman as an area. It
made...it did make me think. That if...I wondered if that
confusion I could see, how much of it was the confusion
of adolescence, the confusion that comes with adolescence
anyway. And I wondered why so many of the transgender
kids seemed to start off in San Francisco. But actually, so
many of those kids hadn't reached adolescence yet. Were
far from adolescence. Like Lila.

But Lila knew what she wanted. And she could read. As soon
as she found out what they were, what was possible, she kept

saying what she wanted. At that stage she was...would have been about about six or seven. She wouldn't leave her mum alone. I suppose you would like me to describe her mum. To describe Karen. So you can judge. Yes. Tanned, high heels. Long hair – Essexy, without being from Essex. Not well off, so takes pleasure from immediate things like magazines. Smokes like me, but not like me. Go on, think it, shallow. So all of our conclusions and prejudices might say that we are not surprised to know, to learn that Karen promised Lila she could have the implants, have boobs when she was older. To wait. And at that stage Lila could get herself a bra from Matalan. A bit big, because Lila was only just seven and the padded bras were supposed to be if you were eight, but Lila would wear it. It seemed like a good compromise. And the tan and the pair of heels seemed like a good compromise too at the time. Karen had long placated Lila with those high-heeled shoes for children that Disney and Dream Dazzlers do, and the lip gloss, make-up bags, glamour gloves with rings, nail varnish, bangles, necklaces and earrings you could get from Toys R Us or eBay or anywhere really, that are made for children from three upwards, although Lila had probably got into them a little earlier, and again, grown out of them earlier and into the more adult-styles of high-heeled shoes for kids. By now Lila had become brilliant at "sexy dancing". She was very good at it. She liked to copy Rihanna to be like a big girl. And she got attention, and she loved the attention, and Karen had to admit she liked the attention Lila got, and sometimes it got her, Karen, additional attention. Though sometimes the tan and the heels on her child got her spat at in the street. And Karen would get shouted at when walking with her daughter. And Lila got called "tanorexic".

When Lila was seven, Karen told me, Lila had what a middle-class mum would call a "play date". Karen was really resourceful about it, maximising Lila's popularity by buying her and her friends a "Pampering Spa Diva Makeover Party" – one of the high-end ones with the "non-alcoholic champagne reception", where they give the little girls fizzy elderflower in flutes and they can have massages and their make-up and nails done and they do a catwalk at the end on a red carpet with floor balloons. If you look them up now, it says "Spa parties for little girls are the *IT* party of 2018". So Karen was well ahead of the game. And they're designed for aged four upwards "to help alleviate the pressure of dating, fitting in with friends and the unfortunate pressure of feeling good about themselves". Anyway, Karen walked in towards the end to find Lila and her friends blushed and curled and glittered, with a magazine shared between them. They were turning the pages and one after another they were saying, "that one, that one" and "that one's nice". And – this is something I just got from Karen, she just mentioned, I couldn't in all honesty say she was dismayed – the thing is, they weren't talking about clothes or even boys, saying "I like that one" and "that one's nice". When Karen looked, what they were talking about were the women's bodies. The women's bodies in the magazine. Which ones they wanted. Who was best. And of course, Lila could go on the internet. And Lila could read. And because the information people want you to want, and what "you may also like" is so accessible, it wasn't long before she could see that you could get them if you wanted: the breasts. And like so many things for us, if you really, really, really want it, that makes it okay. And she worked on her mum.

Karen was aware enough to know that she had to keep it under wraps – that it wasn't legal in this country. At least, she wasn't certain if it was legal, but she thought it probably wasn't – or maybe it was like all those other things that were so new, it was like the Wild West, and there isn't really a law for them yet (people like to call it the Wild West because it sounds romantic and as if they are doing something brave and exciting, and because they always see themselves as the conquerors of the Wild West and not the ones who were damaged or wiped out by it) – and, in any case, Karen was sure it would be frowned upon by some people. Added to all that was the expense. It was so expensive in this country! I mean, yes, you will do anything to fulfil your child's needs and, I mean, God knows how any people do it these days: phones, tablets, trainers, what have you, and "invention is the mother of necessity" as the new saying goes, but you've got to do your best to have them function in the society, and so fulfilling their needs is important, but, even looking at the dodgiest ones in the UK, which Karen was reluctant to do, the operations were really expensive. And Lila wasn't quietening down about this – if anything it was getting worse, and in fact was really starting to distress her – so Karen knew that she would have to look further afield.

The odd thing about Brazil in terms of plastic surgery—

TESSA's *phone rings. The ringtone is the theme tune to* "CAGNEY AND LACEY".

(phone) Oh hi, Ali. How was it? Oh good. Well, don't put it up on my bed this time, leave it on top of the washing machine. Or preferably in it. No, just if you see your dad. No, no. *(it's not important)* No, it was the specialist this time, not the GP. No, no. Just get him to give me a ring. All right darling... Oh that's good. Oh, I might have to get you to set me up with that dictaphone thing. Yep. Ok darling, see you later. Bye.

TESSA *hangs up and puts her phone on the table beside her.*

The odd thing about Brazil in terms of its culture of plastic surgery is that what they see as a positive result over there can be very different to here. They're getting a bit more used to us now as there have now been so many of us travel for ops, but on the whole, in that culture, certainly up until comparatively recently when the whole global market increased, large breasts were seen as something really rather vulgar. I actually even remember treating – I mean it was some years ago now – a British woman who was traumatised following her botched operation. Well actually, that's not fair to say – the operation itself was executed perfectly. She was one of the early pioneers – it was when I'd just started out – and went to have her breast enhancement there. But "enhancement" is a subjective word and at that time, if you were in Brazil, a breast *reduction* was an enhancement. So, imagine her surprise when she went in to have an *enlargement* and woke up to find that she had been given a breast *reduction*? Well. I didn't have to imagine her surprise, I was very much party to it.

The thing was, by the time Lila came along, the surgeries there were much more attuned to our needs. Or requirements, I suppose I should say. And overall, the entire procedure, including the flights, was cheaper than it would have been in this country. Added to that – I mean, Karen's never mentioned it, but her actions tell me it is something she would have been instinctively on guard against – going to South America for the operation meant that any interference from interested parties along the way was minimised. And that when she and her daughter came back the operation would be a fait accompli, and it was.

I suppose you could argue that those same instincts could have pointed her to the fact that there was a moral issue with Lila having the operation, but when you look at Karen, when you question how far her child was sexualised, how far she should have stopped it and how far she contributed to it, when you look at Karen and you see her lack of self-awareness in terms of how far she has been – is – sexualised herself, you do wonder in terms of her responsibility in sexualising her child. How aware could she really be of it as sexual? And not just "fun"? Which, that said, is a trite euphemism we have for sex. You do wonder, until she does something so proactive as giving in to her daughter's demands to buy her a pair of breasts, I suppose. But then, de facto, you enter the whole debate as to whether breasts are sexual organs. Which lots of people who breastfeed in public places or support people who breastfeed in public places would argue they aren't. Primarily. But I'll get on to that more.

I suppose the main thing that strikes me at this stage – I mean, if we're talking about plastic surgery generally – and, perhaps I shouldn't express an opinion, but of course, given my own circumstances, my own little problem, it's something I've considered at length – is that the most basic philosophical question: who am I? We're playing Russian roulette with it, aren't we? Because of the gap. Because the first thing you can do when you ask yourself, "who am I?", is to look in the mirror and see yourself, um...point to who you are. But if then what you see is someone else – even if it's someone you'd like to be or thought you would like to be – there's a gap, isn't there? Between you. Like the mental-health gap between everyone's Facebook profile and themselves as they truly are and are inventing unconsciously from within; and as our identities are something that are constructed from the outside, with the help of a few billion adverts, we are getting frightened to invent unconsciously from within. But don't get me started on that. On our subconscious being stamped out. It's the first philosophical question: who am I? And that's before you even get to a notion of who the society thinks you are. Or when it thinks you stop being a child. Or if it cares.

So Lila had the op – the breast implants. They had a lively time in South America according to Karen. Took the time beforehand to calm down, go to the Amazon, stayed on an eco-resort where Karen and Lila against regulations blew all the power in the lodge by blow-drying their hair. And then Lila had the op, and then they came home. And if you talk to Karen it is clear that she was so worn down that she is proud to have managed to compromise by negotiating down on the cup size from an E to a Double D. Lila had just had her eighth birthday.

I suppose if Karen had been sensible she would have behaved a bit like someone from the witness protection programme and just taken herself and Lila instantly away and given them both a new identity – I mean as far as possible. Obviously she could not have done the full new National Insurance number, credit cards, name etc., but actually there would have been no need. There are cases of children reaching puberty at the age of two – and they are not as rare as you might think. I did my clinical training with a girl whose sister reached puberty at a very early age. And she sometimes talked about how it had affected her family. So. If you came in, new to an area – the British are so appalling at talking about their bodies without embarrassment anyway and hate making personal remarks to anyone's face – you could probably get away with quite a lot in terms of physical extremity if no one knew you. At least for a while. But then how do you manage to keep an eight-year-old in check? An advanced eight-year-old who is incredibly proud of her new breasts? In any case, Karen had not seen any need to turn her life upside down, move house, change schools to accommodate her daughter's wishes, barely anticipating that her life would be turned upside down anyway as a result of them, as all hell broke loose.

Well, I say all hell broke loose, but the reality of it was that it wanted to but it didn't quite know how. I mean, this whole situation, predicament, was entirely unprecedented. When she came in first to school, before it turned to bewilderment and outrage, the teachers were mainly in shock. The other little girls regarded each other darkly with a mixture of tremulousness and awe, as if something at once shameful and extraordinary had happened. They would whisper but at the same time almost form a circle around Lila to create space for her otherness. Some of them were intensely embarrassed, many imagined these new arrivals had developed on their classmate over the holidays and that the same would happen imminently to them, in one of the other breaks. And, as happens naturally and universally in later years, it was embraced by some and dreaded by others. The girl it happens to first is always whispered about and regarded secretly in the moments when you change as a group but hormonal events are beginning their division, and it is as if a new creature is growing in your midst.

The first instinct of the first teacher – a female teacher – to operate proactively in this was to take Lila out of the class, covering her almost as if with one side of her coat like a streaker at a football stadium, and taking her to a small room to sit away on her own secretly, privately with her breasts, where they and she were protected and out of the way. As if they were something to be ashamed of. And as if this atmosphere could be soaked up by Lila as anything other than that they were something to be hidden away, to be ashamed of. And it did make me think of how much, in less direct ways, we give older, less precipitously developing girls this message of shame of these secondary sexual organs, rather than something that just can be out there and left for other people to deal with. In order to protect them. But then, of course, the psychotherapist in me knows that it is not in order to protect them, it is in order to externalise our own shame which we were given at some similar stage, in a similar way.

In an immediate way, for the child, Lila's awareness of herself changed. So much of our self-awareness comes from how we are perceived. It was no longer a game. The lines had become blurred somehow – the public lines anyway – regarding who was to blame if she attracted serious attention. Even though she was eight. As any pop psychology book or simple text book could have preached at Karen and Lila in advance, Lila had these new organs she wasn't emotionally able to cope with. But, excuse my French, that whole idea kind of pisses me off. So the given is, if you have breasts, you ought to be emotionally mature enough to protect them? What are we saying? What about what you were given by nature: are we to take it then that a person who has small breasts is not emotionally mature? A young girl with large breasts should automatically be able to field the reactions of others? And it's her fault if she can't? Because the slightly odd thing seems to have always been that if you have big breasts the overriding opinion seems to be that you are in charge of them somehow. That you must be responsible for

them. Or even that you thought of them yourself. And...
well, I suppose now we can.

Just what exactly did these breasts have planned anyway?
What was their game? And is this changing? Maybe we
have externalised the functionality of our bodies to such an
extent, found so many other ways of doing what our bodies
can do, that they themselves have purely become a luxury.
Like disposable income.

The fact is, when it came to Lila, no one really knew what to
do. The powers that be – any powers that be – were united
in that her mother Karen had abused her in some way, and
I mean, everyone had decided that she was sexualised – by
her mother or had sexualised herself – but, what do you do?
She needed an education. It was another eight years till she
was going to be sixteen and could therefore leave school or
be thrown out. Well. There was lots of discussion amongst
the adults in twos and threes. The head was called. The
mother was called but there had been no response. She must
be at work and not picking up. A bewildered school nurse,
panicked at the invitation of her contribution, involved,
before a doctor was called. And the nature of the doctor
was such that he could only state that Lila was physically
healthy and in no kind of danger from a medical point of
view unless the silicone leaked. Each looked to the other
expectantly to take charge. It was a bit like Officer Krupke.

Once the threat of police was the definite next step, Karen
was forced to take time off work and invited to talk through
all the events leading up to the operation before being told
that the likelihood was that Lila was to be taken into care
and that she, Karen, would be arrested for the emotional
and physical abuse of her child.

Karen wondered if Lila had been born a boy and had been
transgender and had wanted the breasts and been given
them whether the response would have been quite like this
– as opposed to the implicit accusation against Karen for
wanting a mini-me.

Meanwhile, Lila was livid. She didn't want to be locked in a room during school hours, this was not supposed to have been the destiny of her and her new breasts, and the kind of attention that she was getting – from the teachers, the doctor and the social worker, was far from the sort of attention she had had in mind! A large part of her had imagined that her life would change irrevocably as a result of her enhancement – it had but not how she had seen it – she had imagined admiration, adulation even. White fur coats, pulling up in, stepping out of beautiful cars, dancing, adoration from helpless grown men. Living her life in a pop video, the majestic world at her disposal, and she, her flesh, worshipped in soft focus and slow motion. A lot of the time when people imagine being famous, I think they imagine living somewhere like that. I think what they're actually imagining is being someone else entirely.

So Karen was taken into custody and Lila was taken into care. And I am not advocating that she should have been allowed to stay with Karen – obviously a lot of work needed to be done with Karen herself – and I'm not saying this because of the – my – the report, but I do wonder if what happened would have happened if Lila had not been in care.

The press had, of course, been sniffing around from the moment the situation had begun to become slightly public. Inevitably, stories had gone home from school about the girl with breasts in the class and then, on top of the immediate situation, impossible as it was, the teachers and head teachers were having to field parents for whom the line between concerned, nosy, and hysterical was becoming increasingly blurred. I am probably being unfair and it wasn't just to do with Lila being a freakshow for them. I mean, it is natural that you would be concerned. In any case, it was getting round and got around quickly and, of course, it went bonkers on the internet first, before anyone even had time to think of a capital letter to replace Lila's first name, and then the press, who seem to ingest much of their news from social media before ruminating on it, spewing it back into social media and ingesting it again like a fly vomiting to nourish itself, soaked it up as a matter for "public interest". I mean, Christ, aren't the public just interested in anything? So yeah, it was a press dream. They could exploit a fascination with child sexuality whilst at the same time condemning it and ultimately blaming her mum.

At this time, though, the focus did fall mainly on Lila. The—

TESSA's *phone rings.*

(phone) Oh Phil. Yes darling, thanks. No, well it's not definitely bad news. No, we were right.

Yes, as soon as I got in there he got me to put both my arms up and he said there were *two* lumps. So they are going to...he said he will send me for the mammogram. Well, we might be ok, it might be benign. No, it would be a day surgery, just...but they might be benign.

But Phil, look, I might...if it— I know. Yeah, that was really— No that was... There was just one other thing but let's talk face to face. No, it's not— Well, I don't think it's bad, I— What?! Oh God, look you shouldn't be. Well, hang up now till you're out of the car... I— Yeah— I've just got one more patient later. *(Phil has hung up.)* We'll speak when I get home.

TESSA *realises he has gone, hangs up and puts her phone on the table beside her.*

So the effects on Lila were fairly catastrophic. Cameras look fairly different out the other end. And she wasn't meant to be photographed, of course, but she was. And the pictures would be snatched "in the public interest", cameras would be physically fought over, pictures would be rescued and then put up online and then taken down. But not before they had been screen-grabbed. And the people putting them up online would have told themselves that they were doing the right thing, because it was exposing a situation. It bewilders me really, much in the same way that people post pictures of polar bears with sharp biting wire tight round their muzzles, or instruments used to rape women in Nigeria, with one or two words which all say the same, which all say, "Isn't this awful?", whereas actually anyone who disagrees with it, which is most people, don't need – or are even distressed – to see it and anyone who agrees with it is just going to get off on it. But, yeah, we seem to have moved away from "sharing" towards "making people aware". And the pictures of the child with the breasts, they were shared and viewed and Lila was endowed by the viewers with the persona and mind of a woman, but freakish, a satyr, a centaur, an object of fetishism seen to be in charge of her freakishness, owned by herself, and perhaps the only way now left is to be a pin-up. So in some ways at that stage she got her wish. But as any famous person will tell you, if you are a pin-up, you are never there at the time. To experience the love – being the object of love. And it is not unconditional. You are a pin-up because they expect something from you. Something more. Something in the future.

So yes, this extraordinary pin-up was taken from that grey area between public interest and institutionalised paedophilia and appropriated into a darker community.

It's weird, the Dark Web, because there are actually seemingly really innocuous things like Tesco's vouchers sold on there – and their link might be right next to one selling passports or exams certificates or, of course, some of the most sinister of websites that the Dark Web is notorious for. Anyway, it would have been circulated on there. And, of course, this is the worry when people post pictures of their children online, that they will be circulated in a particular community, that the child could be tracked down. And given her unusual nature – nature perhaps being an obtuse word of me to choose – Lila was more easily tracked down than most.

And people were doing the most extraordinary gymnastics to get her to send them selfies. Lila doing selfies, no concept of what the impact and implications might be. There were

several arrests. If you are over the age of thirteen it is against
the law to send or receive an indecent picture of a person
under the age of eighteen. This includes sending a picture of
yourself, but since Lila was under thirteen it didn't apply to
her and she wasn't doing anything illegal. Nor, of course, is
any child under thirteen who gets groomed or coerced into
sending a picture of themselves. Many of the arrests were
adolescent boys who claimed they didn't know it was illegal
to receive/possess the pictures of Lila. Well, I suppose it was
so rampant and present in the papers in every other possible
way, why would they? And many of them weren't adolescent
boys and couldn't be traced. And, it was not difficult to say
enough to Lila to get her to send a picture. That is one of
the things she had in common with some of the other girls
in the care home from the start. Mainly the ones who were
a *little* bit older to be fair. And it was, you know, it was hard
for the authorities. They tried to confiscate it, but a phone
has basically become a human right. They sort of had to
wait until the money – Karen's money – on it ran out, in
the knowledge that, at any moment, an obliging shadowy
figure might attempt to gain access to Lila and give her a
phone as a present. I think in the end a resourceful care
worker permanently misplaced the charger. And throughout
all of this there were those who believed the whole thing to
be an elaborate hoax and the Lila pics to be nothing more
than an audacious feat of Photoshop.

So. It was while all this was unfolding, and she had been
under arrest, that Karen and I were first introduced. And
it was then, in some respect, that Karen reluctantly began
her work with me – though obviously the nature of our
goals was slightly different at that time than it is now. It
was before the trial and with a view to it, and I think it is
fair to say that at the beginning, although it was interesting
to me, I wasn't "involved". I wasn't how you see me now. I
became more so as the sessions went on and the time went
on and the case was prepared. I was put to work with her
and provide an expert witness report, but at the same time

she was undergoing interviews with a psychiatrist too, who
was to assess whether there was a more concrete clinical
diagnosis to be made. Whether there was a psychosis or
anything like that. They consulted both of us. The initial
job had been in connection with the social services and the
decision to put Lila in care. Karen's most overriding and
immediate issue that I could see was, of course, acute grief
over the separation from her child.

The case began, and there was media interest, and with the
evidence gradually...very gradually it was starting to look
as if Karen might not be jailed, and then, just as it looked
as though it was going to go through, almost as if someone
had taken a cue, the unthinkable happened.

TESSA *pauses to breathe.*

It still makes me furious that the press described the rape
of Lila as "inevitable". Why? Why inevitable?

I'm not going to go into it, if you want to know exactly how
it happened you can go on Google or refer back to the more
prurient papers who recounted events with the horrified glee
that only "respect for the public interest" can demand. It's
likely it can be traced back to being facilitated though not
directly perpetrated by a worker in the care facility itself.
And the cynic in me wonders how long that had been a
less high-profile racket for them before Lila. It was awful.
Apart from the horrific nature of the incident itself, it was
everywhere. There was no possible way of keeping it from
Karen, or fielding it or softening it for her, and just as Karen's
distress over her child reached its height, the vilification of
her, the mother, became its most intense.

In the days on the way to her trial, Karen was hounded,
properly spat at now by mobs of people in large numbers,
cloak over the head, taken off in a van, throngs of press
photographers with periscope arms stretching up and
flashing at the windows as she was driven off round a corner
at a screech, the whole bit.

We have a very unhealthy and frightening addiction to "I told you so" in this country. Because now the dangerous and wrong thing was that people felt justified that they could say, even that they could believe, that if she hadn't had the breasts it wouldn't have happened, that because Lila had the breasts there was a "reason" for her to have been pursued and rooted out like this. And we all know how near a relative of the "reason" is the "excuse". And this is just so...so – I don't even know where to begin.

As misfortune would have it, at this raw and vulnerable time – during an afternoon adjournment – I overheard a person voice as much, in, of all places, that bastion of British civility, Marks & Spencer's.

"So what are you saying?" I heard myself bark at her. (Nobody thinks that someone who doesn't know them will challenge them publicly out of the blue on expressing an opinion and she looked nonplussed.) "Yes, you. What are you saying, that just because someone has breasts they are asking to be violated?"

She cleared her throat and just stared.

"What if someone is out breastfeeding their baby, are they asking for it?"

The woman stared at me before her slow and deliberate reply: "That girl's breasts aren't functional. Except for the obvious."

"I am not talking about her breasts, I am talking about any breasts. And anyway, I think her breasts are not sexual organs either—"

"Well, they obviously are! That's why she wanted them in the first place!...I think you know what I mean", said the woman, evenly. "And it is not unreasonable to hold the mother in some ways responsible."

"What if there hadn't been a mother involved? What would you have called it then?"

"What?"

"And who else is responsible? Who?"

The woman started to edge away. "The man, men obviously."

"And who else?"

"Oh, for God's sake!"

And the irritated woman moved away to continue her shopping elsewhere and a velvety voice behind me said, "Excuse me, madam, did you just say breasts?", and the security guard to whom it belonged escorted me from the premises.

At this point I was surprised to realise I was scared. It did look as if Karen might go to prison. And I realised I thought that was wrong. What do you do with that bit of a female child that wants to be a woman? That sees how it can help her be noticed and loved? In this world? So ok. Here's my opinion. I shouldn't give an opinion. So this is between you and me. Some people, like Karen, facilitate the expression of it. And are probably misguided. But how many more people exploit it? And go unquestioned. Or even facilitated themselves. Look, I don't know if I did think it was wrong – actually, I don't care about right or wrong and have never understood them. I just didn't think it was helpful, would have been helpful. For her to be jailed. I don't think it would have been helpful for anyone.

So it went on, the trial. Karen went on the stand. There she was trying to explain what it was, how it had come about, what she was. Trying to convince the world she was "a mum". But the people had already decided really. They were baying for the notion of childhood innocence and so the mother was vilified for sexualising her child, and, you know, the public were not even sympathetic to the child herself for offending it. Almost veering towards thinking of Lila in the same way they might think of Mary Bell or Thompson and Venables or the Hartlepool girls who bludgeoned Angela

Wrightson, – for her cold-blooded murder of the ideal of the innocent child.

I won't dwell on how long we waited, and the events of the intervening months it dragged on for, how it was touch and go, but once the court had concluded, as I said before, that the law could not formally punish her, cosmetic procedures for children not being illegal, the job was, they needed to be able to portray her, Karen, as an aberration. And this is where I came in. Because. I am...what I actually do, I work with realigning people with society. I am a doctor. And yes, it's mainly women, especially those who have suffered some sort of sexual or identity trauma. So you can see how Karen at first wasn't a willing participant in all this. But treatment had to be seen to be done and we've been, you know, we've been...working. And Karen is in an enclosed facility that isn't a prison. And we continue. And someone else is working with Lila, someone who specialises with children with this sort of thing. Not that there was a "this sort of thing" until now.

So now. Lila, where are we. She's twelve now. Well, she's got social workers, child psychologists coming out of her ears now. I have access to the notes as the mother is in treatment with me. Lila is being treated for trauma – has been since the assault, and as far as the other thing is concerned, of course, almost immediately, right from the moment she and her mum were apprehended was mooted the idea of a reduction. Breast reduction. Breasts, what we were originally talking about. A reversal of the operation continues to be discussed. But Lila...the thing is she does not actually want that. So, although the law has concluded that her mother physically abused Lila, or, at the very least, subjected her to abuse or enabled it, the question is: who do the breasts belong to? Whose *is* Lila's body now? Where are we, ethically, enforcing an operation, a breast reduction, on a child who does not want one? It is not like ordinary healing. I mean, it is not a million miles away from the ethical dilemma of whether you should force a child who's a Christian Scientist to have a blood transfusion. What do we do, do we wait until the therapists and counsellors and social workers have reached a stage with her where she will agree to the reduction? Where are we legally with that? The thing is, the fact is, that by the time it has gone through – all the debate, any ruling about an operation, she will probably have reached an age where her friends will have caught up with her – when she would be developing naturally anyway. I suppose the question then will be, how will she respond to not being different or special anymore? Maybe she will develop something else, but, as even the most conservative fading beauty will tell you, it is not always easy when you have relied on something like that.

So the mind doctors are treating her, the social workers working on her. Trying to get Lila to comprehend, to agree that the healthiest course would be to consent to the reversal, and the odd sort of sick irony is that because of the timing they are almost working in direct opposition to the course of adolescence through which nature will soon require her to become a sexual being anyway.

And, as far as the publicity is concerned, it is now as if the media, the PR world, the papers are lying in wait for the day that she reaches sixteen. There is a stand-off between the law waiting to enforce a reduction and the society waiting for her age to catch up with her. It reminds me of how they were with Emma Watson from *Harry Potter*, lying in wait for her to become sixteen to legitimately unleash. Which was always interesting in itself, and the fact that Watson's stardom originated through a set of children's books and films puts it on the slightly sinister side of interesting... wouldn't you say?

Lila will never not be the girl who had a breast enhancement at the age of eight. In twenty, thirty years' time she will be on television or whatever will be the equivalent of the day and signing autographs with the same vapid resignation that

David Soul signs *Starsky & Hutch* posters forty years on as if playing Kenneth Hutch happened to him and nothing else.

You see, the more we go on, I wonder how much more work will have to be done with people like Lila. And Karen. Before it becomes a social...before it becomes maybe something we have to look at. Because of all the advertising. And more. What they are asking me to fight is a hair's breadth away from the norm, from reality, or at least one of them, because now we have two realities going on and constantly feeding into each other at least.

At the moment it suits us to look at it and her, Karen, as an aberration. As a rogue and random flood rather than a signal of climate change. The thing that worries me is if we just see it, force it to be an anomaly, then we won't...do anything. About the wider picture.

We have talked a lot about "freedom", Karen and I. Lila's choice. Karen's choice: "My choice for my child". When I asked her, "Do you see it that your child belongs to you?", she went silent.

I believe you only have the choices you can see.

Obviously her age is the...Lila's age is a shocking thing. But overall. I have to say, it doesn't surprise me that that is what girls are wanting. That their evolutionary goal might now be to compete with the virtual woman. When I talk to PSHE teachers – sorry that's personal, social and health education – they don't have it in every school – once you have got over the complaint that most of the time they would like to spend teaching is taken up dealing with the effects of social media and cyberbullying, the main thing they have noticed in the last couple of years is the rise in female pupils quizzing them about internet pornography. Almost as if they were trying to suss out what the competition is. What should they be? How do they reconcile this with what they might have liked to be themselves? And is it possible?

And the sad thing is, what they don't realise is that for the inadequate man (and what boy isn't an inadequate man?), the virtual woman will win every time because if a woman doesn't have any emotional needs he can't fail. So then what will happen? Will the girls suppress their emotional needs? What will happen then? Maybe once people start to embrace more fully the negative impact on boys' and young men's neurological development, something might be done about it. Or if there starts being a way it doesn't make money anymore, perhaps. Or maybe our state of affairs will just skip the cliché stage and start to become a "Universal Truth".

You see, you know the thing is, what it boiled down to, Lila just wanted to be a big girl. She wanted to be grown up. And that's normal, it's always been normal. But it's what that is, what that involves, it's "the jungle out there" that has changed. And it's the same reason, paradoxically, that we've got the odd teenager buying Botox, and the same reason that there are little girls of eleven with STIs. And I'm not sure how much I can...you see, speaking for myself, I'm not sure I have the skills. I'm not sure I can help people to be happy, or not sad, or function (TESSA's *phone rings.*) in the jungle.

(phone) Oh hi. No, they've not arrived yet. Well, ok, if— Can't you wait till I get home? Ok, I don't mind talking about it over the phone. It's, um...look Phil. I'm jumping the gun... I don't want to...I don't want the...if it goes ahead, I've already said I don't want chemotherapy, but also...if they take it...I don't want to *(She can't say it.)* have the reconstructive surgery; I've decided. Yeah. I'm not going to ask you if you're ok with that because it's my body. *(roars laughing)* I thought you'd say that. Yep. Yes Phil. Maybe you're right!

(A buzzer sounds. At the same time Phil cuts out.)

Yes, Synchronicity. (TESSA *realises he's gone and hangs up*) Good old Mr Jung.

As the lights gradually go down **TESSA** *unscrews her electronic cigarette.*

The buzzer sounds again.

SUGGESTED CUTS FOR EDINBURGH ONE HOUR VERSION

Page 1
Cut: 'Having to. Make space for them.'
Cut: '...really. I suppose if I was young there would be some debate about the advertising and whether that got me into it. Because everyone's protecting the young. Well, "meatily" if not virtually. So yeah. These are meant to be good. I mean, they are good. There's a lot of talk about whether they are actually promoting them as a health thing over this side of the world in order to support the tobacco industry elsewhere. Because while the tobacco industry has its healthy cut of the healthy electronic market over here, cigarettes are being sold to kids to Africa. Their cigarettes. Sometimes one at a time. Supporting itself by looking good in one area. Fucking Peter to make love to Paul, you could say. It relies on having the life-long customer.'
Add: 'Not that this is. But,' yeah, it's just my way of relaxing.
Cut: '...really. You can't get all moral about it. Well, you can.'

Page 2
Cut: 'I've just been dealing with the mother.'

Page 3:
Cut: 'When she came, it had already got really big. You maybe know about it all anyway, but some of you might not, so I suppose I will tell you.'
Replace: 'I suppose, well...' *with* 'it's not like it hasn't been discussed on "Newsnight", so' ...let's just say...
Cut: 'I'm going to have to talk about this sometime. I will have to write another report. I will probably have to speak to the press or at least be quoted in the press at some point, and, who knows, if I ever start giving lectures, we'll call her Lila and Karen might be an important case study, or an experience for the novel, so... best if I process it with you. Why not.'
Cut: 'She was lively and intelligent. Precocious in some ways, Lila, according to Karen. Karen is her mum. Was her mum. I'm treating Karen, did I mention that? Because I have to. So, yeah, so.'

Page 4:
Cut: 'Anyway, like I say, he was probably slightly coming out the other side of realising he would never be a rock star and starting to mourn it.'

Page 5:
Cut: 'A man about the house pointing in her direction was a matter for celebration. A raven-haired, swarthy man with the embers of his inner rock star still glowing near the surface, a matter for euphoria.'

Page 6:
Cut: 'People used to say to a novelist friend, why have you got trains and railways all the way through all your work and, you know, she hadn't realised, hadn't consciously made it a motif, but she had been brought up in a commuter town near a station, and the trains were part of her emotional backdrop, so there you go.'

Page 7:
Cut: 'But let's not get too analytical, I'm getting ahead of myself here. At first Karen thought she, Lila, was just pointing at the page. And, I mean that's what it would have looked like. Just a child ham-fistedly, unspecifically pawing at a random page, at a picture. You wouldn't particularly notice that what she was pointing at all had one thing in common. I mean, not unless you were looking. And not unless it became emphatic which, after a while, it did.'

Page 8:
Cut: 'A bit like that *Little Britain* character who kept saying "bitty" to his mum. What a grim comparison that is, actually. So she kept pointing; she knew what she wanted, like they do.'
Cut: 'her whole small being was involved...'
Cut: 'Make placating sounds for her daughter. Try to get on with her own thing, which was rapidly no thing and no longer her own, try to work.'

Page 9:
Cut: 'Oh, I should say, when Lila was just about four, she became brilliant at sexy dancing. It seemed slightly odd because it happened literally overnight – well, over a day. Lila's little friend had MTV at his house. The child Karen dropped off in the morning could do only little elbowy hands-and-knees and side-to-side dancing, and the child she went to pick up late that afternoon was rubbing down her torso with her imaginary long-fingernailed hands and grinding her figmental-thonged hips. I mean, in a way it shouldn't be odd because dancers can just

learn dances, people can just pick up dances, ways of moving, can't they? And Lila had just picked it up off the telly. And at the time the mums had laughed! Karen and Lila's friend's mum had laughed because it was funny, because she was so good at it, and it looked like an idea. At least it did to them.'

Page 10:
Cut: 'Not that it was at all straightforward. So some of the children were injected and treated before they became women or men, so that they could grow into men or women.'

Page 11:
Cut: 'Karen had long placated Lila with those high-heeled shoes for children that Disney and Dream Dazzlers do, and the lip gloss, make-up bags, glamour gloves with rings, nail varnish, bangles, necklaces and earrings you could get from Toys R Us or eBay or anywhere really, that are made for children from three upwards, although Lila had probably got into them a little earlier, and again, grown out of them earlier and into the more adult-styles of high-heeled shoes for kids.'

Page 15:
Cut: '...behaved a bit like someone from the witness protection programme and...'
Cut: '...and given them both a new identity – I mean as far as possible. Obviously she could not have done the full new National Insurance number, credit cards, name etc., but actually there would have been no need.'

Page 16:
Cut: 'And she sometimes talked about how it had affected her family.'
Cut: 'I mean, this whole situation, predicament, was entirely unprecedented.'
Add: ...embarrassed, many 'supposed'...
Cut: '...imagined these new arrivals had developed on their classmate over the holidays and...'
Cut: '...whispered about and...'

Page 17:
Cut: '– a female teacher –'
Cut: 'almost as if with one side of her coat...'
Cut: 'And as if this atmosphere could be soaked up by Lila as

anything other than that they were something to be hidden away, to be ashamed of.'

Cut: 'So much of our self-awareness comes from how we are perceived.'

Page 18:

Cut: 'And is this changing? Maybe we have externalised the functionality of our bodies to such an extent, found so many other ways of doing what our bodies can do, that they themselves have purely become a luxury. Like disposable income. The fact is, when it came to Lila...really...'

Add: ...everyone had decided that 'Lila' was sexualised...

Cut: '– by her mother or had sexualised herself –'

Cut: 'She needed an education.'

Replace: 'Karen was forced to take time off work and invited to talk' *with* 'Karen was forced to take time off and invited in to talk'

Add: ...been given them 'if' the response...

Page 19:

Cut: 'She didn't want to be locked in a room during school hours.'

Cut: '...it had but not how she had seen it –'

Cut: 'I think they imagine living somewhere like that'

Cut: 'I am probably being unfair and it wasn't just to do with Lila being a freakshow for them. I mean, it is natural that you would be concerned. In any case,'

Page 21:

Cut: '...whereas actually anyone who disagrees with it, which is most people, don't need – or are even distressed – to see it and anyone who agrees with it is just going to get off on it.'

Page 23:

Cut: 'They consulted both of us.'

Page 24:

Replace: 'We have a very unhealthy and frightening addiction to "I told you so" in this country. Because' *with* 'And'

Replace: 'And anyway, I think her breasts are not sexual organs either—' *with* 'So, what? They are just there for other people to gawp at?'

Cut: '...I think you know what I mean", said the woman, evenly.'

Page 26:
Cut: So 'now.' Lila, 'where are we.'
Replace: 'although the law has concluded that her mother physically abused Lila, or at the very least, subjected her to abuse or enabled it...' *with* '...so the question now is:'
Cut: 'It is not like ordinary healing.'

Page 27:
Cut: 'So the mind doctors are treating her, the social workers working on her. Trying to get Lila to comprehend, to agree that the healthiest course would be to consent to the reversal, and the odd sort of sick irony is that because of the timing they are almost working in direct opposition to the course of adolescence through which nature will soon require her to become a sexual being anyway.'
Cut: 'as far as the publicity is concerned'
Cut: 'from *Harry Potter*'

Page 28:
Cut: 'Before it becomes a social...before it becomes maybe something we have to look at.'
Replace 'What they are asking me to fight is a hair's breadth away from the norm, from reality, or at least one of them, because now we have two realities going on and constantly feeding into each other at least. At the moment it suits us to look at it and her, Karen, as an aberration. As a rogue and random flood rather than a signal of climate change. The thing that worries me is if we just see it, force it to be an anomaly, then we won't...do anything. About the wider picture.' *with* 'At the moment it suits us to look at it and her, Karen, as an aberration. As a rogue and random flood rather than a signal of climate change. But what they are asking me to fight is a hairs breadth away from the norm, from reality, or at least one of them because now we have 2 realities going on and constantly feeding into each other at least.'
Cut: 'And is it possible?'

Page 29:
Cut: 'if they take it'

Page 30:
Move stage direction: (*A buzzer sounds. At the same time Phil cuts out.*) *to after* 'Yes, Synchronicity.'

FURNITURE AND PROPERTY LIST

<u>Furniture:</u>
Chair
Small side-table

<u>Props:</u>
TESSA's phone
TESSA's large handbag
A nicotine-free electronic cigarette/shisha pen
A glasses case
A glass of "whisky" or a mug of tea

LIGHTING PLOT

A simple pool of light

EFFECTS PLOT

"Cagney and Lacey" ringtone
Buzzer (doctor's)

THIS
IS
NOT
THE
END

Lightning Source UK Ltd.
Milton Keynes UK
UKOW01f1412020218
317286UK00001B/6/P